Lost Railways of
Co. Tyrone and Co. Fermanagh

by
Stephen Johnson

A double-headed northbound GNR(I) train led by PPs Class
4-4-0 No. 46, 'Typhoon', at Victoria Bridge Station.

PICTURE ACKNOWLEDGEMENTS
The publishers wish to thank the following for contributing pictures to this book: John Alsop for pages 33 and 44; R.M. Casserley for the inside front cover, pages 2, 4, 5, 7, 8, 12, 13, 18, 19, 22, 26, 28, 29, 32, 34, 35, 37–41, 46 and 48 (all of these photographs were taken by H.C. Casserley); Ian McCullough for pages 1, 9, 10, 14–16, 20, 21, 23, 25, 27, 30, 31, 45, 47 and the inside back cover; W.A.C. Smith for pages 6, 11 and 17 (these photographs were taken by W.A.C. Smith); Des Quail for the front cover and pages 36, 42, and 43. The pictures on pages 24 and the back cover are from the publishers' collection.

Trew & Moy Station, 13 June 1964.

INTRODUCTION

The counties of Tyrone and Fermanagh once had an extensive railway network of both broad and narrow gauge lines, but sadly there are none left. Two major routes made their way through these counties, both operated by the Great Northern Railway of Ireland. The first was the sprawling Irish North route from Dundalk to Londonderry which was built up in sections over a period by a number of different companies. The second was the Derry Road which offered an alternative route from Belfast to Londonderry to that offered by the remaining Northern Counties Committee route via Coleraine. From a junction at Portadown, the Derry Road, as the line became known, went via Dungannon and Pomeroy before meeting the Irish North at Omagh.

A branch off the Irish North served the popular resort of Bundoran, whereas another, to Fintona, was formed when the southward extension of the route bypassed the town. This three-quarter mile stub is perhaps best remembered for its tram. For 104 years until closure, the line was worked by horse tram, in latter years pulled by a horse called Dick. Fortunately the tramcar survives in a museum. Another branch served Cookstown, leaving the Derry Road at Dungannon. This line went through the industrial area of Coalisland before terminating at a station adjacent to the NCC station in the town. Although through running wasn't possible, an exchange siding was provided for wagon transfers.

The GNR(I) remained independent until closure. The reason for this was the partition of the country in 1921. All lines operating wholly within the Irish Free State became absorbed in the Great Southern Railways company, eventually to become CIE, whereas all those operating in the north eventually came under the control of the Ulster Transport Authority. Those lines that crossed over the international border remained independent. This ultimately caused the demise of these railways as natural traffic flows were disrupted and customs checks hindered traffic – the GNR(I) crossed the border no less than seventeen times! The financial difficulties that beset the GNR(I) from the 1930s came to a head in the 1950s when the company had to be bailed out by the governments of the two countries and the Great Northern Railway Board was established in 1953. Disagreement over funding of the GNRB led to the Northern Government withdrawing from the agreement and this resulted in closure of parts of the GNRB network and the splitting of the remainder of the company between the UTA and CIE in 1958. CIE were left with various stubs which were patently unworkable and these were closed in the 1960s. The quirky and independent Sligo, Leitrim & Northern Counties Railway were a casualty of this situation. Running from Sligo to Enniskillen, the company had no option but to close when the former Irish North route was closed in 1957. With the connection at Enniskillen gone, the company found that they would be running a railway to nowhere.

The narrow gauge railways suffered a different fate. The Castlederg & Victoria Bridge Tramway, always an impecunious affair, gave up after the Railway Strike of 1933. The Clogher Valley Railway managed to soldier on to 1941. Although this company operated entirely in the north, the major companies declined to purchase it. It therefore remained independent, being assisted by county council grants until closure. The Donegal Railway Company built an extension from Strabane to Londonderry, opening in 1900. After the joint purchase of the company by the English Midland Railway's Northern Counties Committee and the GNR(I), the Government handed this extension to the NCC in order to avoid a monopoly of the route by the GNR(I). This line ultimately ended up under UTA control and was promptly closed.

In this book the Irish North route is examined first, followed by the Derry Road and then the GNR(I)'s branch lines. The independent narrow gauge lines of counties Tyrone and Fermanagh follow before attention is turned to the unique Sligo, Leitrim & Northern Counties Railway where locomotives were not numbered and were known by names only.

COOKSTOWN P27

Clones – Strabane

Passenger service withdrawn 1 October 1957 (Clones to Omagh) / 15 February 1965 (Omagh to Strabane)

Distance 67.25 miles

Company Great Northern Railway of Ireland

Stations closed	*Date*
Clones *	14 October 1957
Clonmaulin Crossing **	1940s
Newtownbutler	1 October 1957
Lisnanock Crossing **	1940s
Sallaghy Crossing **	1940s
Keady Crossing **	1940s
Aughalurcher Crossing **	1940s
Killynamph Crossing **	1940s
Castlebalfour Crossing **	1940s

Stations closed	*Date*
Barnhill Crossing **	1940s
Lisnaskea	1 October 1957
Lisnagole Crossing **	1940s
Aughnaskew Crossing **	1940s
Maguiresbridge ***	1 October 1957
Kilnashambally Crossing **	1940s
Coolane Crossing **	1940s
Lisbellaw	1 October 1957
Ballylucas Crossing **	1 October 1957
Enniskillen (old station)	1860
Enniskillen (new station) ****	1 October 1957
Drumclay Crossing **	1940s
Gortaloughan Halt *****	1 October 1957

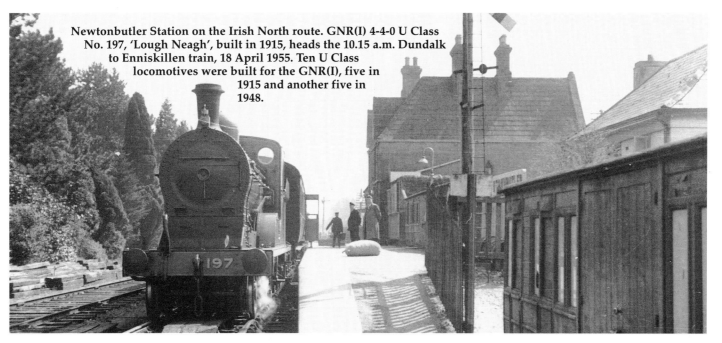

Newtonbutler Station on the Irish North route. GNR(I) 4-4-0 U Class No. 197, 'Lough Neagh', built in 1915, heads the 10.15 a.m. Dundalk to Enniskillen train, 18 April 1955. Ten U Class locomotives were built for the GNR(I), five in 1915 and another five in 1948.

* Closed to northbound trains on 1 October 1957; remained open until 14 October 1957 for the train from Dundalk and Cavan.
** Railcar stop from 1935.
*** Opened on 1 March 1859.
**** Opened in 1860 to replace old station.
***** Opened in 1940.

Clones – Strabane (continued)

Stations closed	Date	Stations closed	Date
Drumcullion Halt *	1 October 1957	Togher Crossing **	1940s
Drumsonnis Crossing **	1940s	Kiltamnagh Crossing **	1940s
Ballinamallard	1 October 1957	Edergole Upper Crossing **	1940s
Bundoran Junction ***	1 October 1957	Culmore Crossing **	1940s
Loughterush Crossing **	1940s	Omagh (new station) *****	15 February 1965
Trillick ****	1 October 1957	Omagh (old station)	1863
Shanmullagh Crossing **	1 October 1957	Mountjoy Halt †	1935
Galbally Crossing **	1940s	Newtownstewart	15 February 1965
Dromore Road	1 October 1957	Victoria Bridge	15 February 1965
Lissaneden Crossing **	1940s	Trafalgar ††	date unknown
Racrane Crossing **	1940s	Sion Mills	15 February 1965
Fintona Junction	1 October 1957	Strabane	15 February 1965

* Opened during the 1940s as an unadvertised halt serving the seaplane base on Lower Lough Erne.
** Railcar stop from 1935.
*** Called Lowtherstown Road from 1854 to 1861, then Irvinestown from 1861 to 1863, and Irvinestown Road from 1863 to 1866.
**** Closed for a period by the INWR.
***** Opened in 1863.
† Open from 1852 to 1859, 1870 to 1878, and 1928 to 1935.
†† Private station, dates unknown.

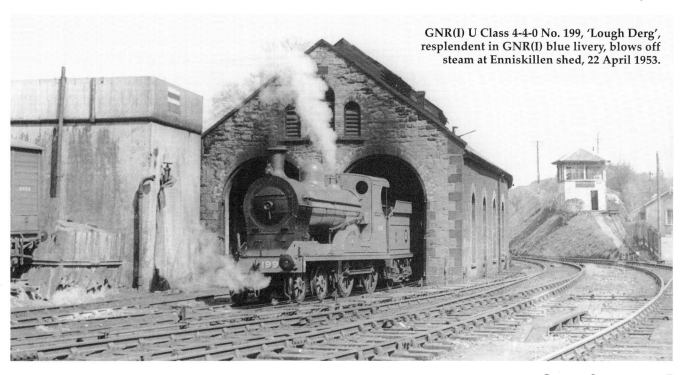

GNR(I) U Class 4-4-0 No. 199, 'Lough Derg', resplendent in GNR(I) blue livery, blows off steam at Enniskillen shed, 22 April 1953.

GNR(I) PPs Class 4-4-0 No. 12, pictured on 21 September 1957 with the 6.40 p.m. service to Omagh at Enniskillen, an important station where the SNLCR met the GNR(I).

This line was part of a larger route from Dundalk to Londonderry, the building of which involved three companies and a considerable amount of time. The line had started with the Dundalk & Western Railway in 1837, with the first sod cut at Dundalk amid great ceremony in 1839. However, nothing happened after this and the scheme was abandoned for a number of years. It was resurrected on 21 July 1845 with the incorporation of the Dundalk & Enniskillen Railway. Although construction started on 15 October 1845, progress was slow and despite its title the company only got as far Clones. The intention was to share the costs and responsibilities of the remainder of the line from Clones to Enniskillen with the Newry & Enniskillen Railway, but as it happened the poorly run N&ER didn't get anywhere near Clones or Enniskillen so the powers were transferred to the D&ER. The line was opened in sections from Dundalk, with Clones and Lisnaskea being reached on 7 July 1858. Construction continued and the section from Lisnaskea to Lisbellaw opened on 16 August 1858, with the final section to Enniskillen being opened on 15 February 1859.

GNR(I) PPs Class 4-4-0 No. 43, 'Lagan', at Bundoran Junction Station with the 11.15 a.m. Londonderry to Dundalk service, 19 September 1929. The junction formed a triangle with platforms on two sides of the triangle.

The third company involved was the Londonderry & Enniskillen Railway. Incorporated in July 1845, this was authorised to build a line from Londonderry to Enniskillen via Strabane and Omagh. Construction started in October 1845, with the first section to Strabane down the west bank of the River Foyle being completed and opened on the 19 April 1847. The siting of the Londonderry terminus was subject to some difference of opinion and was originally built at Gallows Strand. This site was found to be somewhat inconvenient and an extension, opening on 18 April 1850, was made towards the city to a site just south of the Carlisle Bridge, known as Foyle Road from 1904. Initial results were so poor that in 1848, the L&ER board tried to abandon the rest of the line. However, the company carried on pushing southwards with sections of the line opening in stages. Strabane to Newtownstewart opened on 9 May 1852 and Omagh was reached on 13 September 1852. The next section was built to the small town of Fintona and opened on 15 June 1853. However, when the line was built towards Dromore Road, it commenced not from Fintona but from a junction three quarters of a mile further north at a location later known as Fintona Junction. The section to Dromore Road duly opened on 16 January 1854. The remaining part of the line from Dromore Road to Enniskillen opened on 19 August 1854.

Fintona Junction, 19 September 1929, with the tram ready for the three-quarter mile journey down to Fintona. This was the easy part of the journey for the horse as it was all downhill.

When the two companies met at Enniskillen in 1859, initially the L&ER station was used until the D&ER built a replacement which opened in 1860. It soon became apparent to the board of the L&ER that the complete route would be better run as one concern, so from 1 January 1860 they leased their line to the D&ER for ninety-nine years. To reflect their new responsibilities the D&ER changed its name to the Irish North Western Railway by Act of Parliament on 7 July 1862. In the meantime, the Portadown, Dungannon & Omagh Railway had reached Omagh, opening their line on 2 September 1861. This new line offered an alternative route from Belfast to Londonderry and initially used the L&ER station. A new station was built at the junction, opening in 1863. Also, in 1861, a new company, the Enniskillen & Bundoran Railway, was empowered to build a line from a junction at Lowtherstown on the L&ER to Bundoran. This opened on 13 June 1866, by which time Lowtherstown had become Bundoran Junction. A direct curve was opened in 1894 to allow trains from the Omagh direction to gain access to the branch without reversal.

Omagh Station, looking south. The Derry Road can be seen curving away to the left while the Irish North route curves to the right. Although the latter closed in 1957, Omagh retained the Londonderry–Belfast service until 1965.

On 7 September 1863 the Finn Valley Railway opened their broad gauge line from Strabane to Stranolar. The FVR made a junction with the L&ER just to the south of the station, which was shared. This arrangement continued until 16 July 1894 when the company, now called the Donegal Railway, built its own station adjacent to the GNR(I) station and re-gauged their line to 3 feet gauge. 1875 saw the formation of the Northern Railway of Ireland and the INWR joined the fold on 1 January 1876, the L&ER remaining independent for the time being. However, the lease that the L&ER had given the INWR was transferred to the NR(I). The NR(I) was a short-lived company, ending on 1 April 1876 when the Ulster Railway amalgamated to form the Great Northern Railway of Ireland. The Sligo, Leitrim & Northern Counties Railway started to build their railway from Enniskillen towards Sligo in 1877, starting at Enniskillen. The first section of line opened for goods on 12 February 1879, with passenger traffic following on 18 March 1879. Although a connection to the GNR(I) was provided for wagon transfer, the SLNCR used a temporary station until agreement was reached with the GNR(I) over the junction layout. A bay platform was provided and SLNCR trains used the GNR(I) station from 1883.

Newtonstewart Station, some ten miles north of Omagh, closed in 1965.

The still independent L&ER eventually promoted a Bill for amalgamation with the GNR(I) and joined the fold in 1883. On 10 July 1884 the Castlederg & Victoria Bridge Tramway opened. This 3 feet gauge roadside tramway terminated behind the down platform of the GNR(I) Victoria Bridge Station. The Clogher Valley Tramway had been building their line from Tynan through south Tyrone in 1885. The 3 feet gauge CVR met the GNR(I) at Maguiresbridge, opening for traffic on 2 May 1887. Partition in 1921 caused numerous problems for the GNR(I), the line commencing in the Irish Free State and terminating in Northern Ireland. Along the way, the line crossed the state border three times, at Clones, Strabane and Carrigans. Customs posts were set up at Clones in the Irish Free State and Newtownbutler in Northern Ireland. The 1920s also heralded another threat to the line in the form of competing road transport. Profits began to fall, becoming a loss in 1933. The Railway Strike of 1933 didn't help matters and the GNR(I) looked for economies. One of these was in the form of railcars, introduced on the line in 1935. As well as serving the established stations, the railcars would also stop at numerous level crossings in an effort to pick up extra traffic.

GNR(I) S Class 4-4-0 No. 174, 'Carrantuohill', at Strabane Station with the 3.50 p.m. service from Londonderry to Belfast, 3 April 1956. Two companies served Strabane – the GNR(I) and the narrow gauge Co. Donegal, whose station was reached by the footbridge.

The Second World War saw the economic situation improve for the GNR(I), but caused problems for this particular line. Since it crossed the state border, War Department traffic would have had to pass through neutral Éire on its way to the major naval base at Londonderry so this traffic went on the NCC route via Coleraine instead. The immediate post-war years saw a return to financial difficulties. In 1953 the governments of the two countries set up the Great Northern Railway Board, underwriting the losses of the railway. In 1956, the Northern Minister of Commerce proposed a radical closure programme, including the Omagh to Newtownbutler section of the Irish North. Although these proposals were initially opposed, a public enquiry was held and the outcome revealed that minimal savings would be achieved. Nonetheless, the Minister of Commerce stated his intention to proceed with the closures and services ceased at the end of September 1957. All services between Clones and Omagh ended on 1 October 1957. This still left the Omagh to Londonderry section in use as part of the route from Belfast to Londonderry via Portadown. A year later the GNRB ceased to exist from midnight on 30 September 1958.

Strabane, 20 April 1948. GNR(I) PPs Class 4-4-0 No. 106, 'Tornado', stands to the left next to the narrow gauge station while Qs Class 4-4-0 No. 121, 'Pluto', heads the 9.25 a.m. Londonderry to Belfast train.

The Ulster Transport Authority acquired the assets in Northern Ireland and continued to operate services over the remaining part of the line between Omagh and Londonderry until it finally closed the Portadown to Londonderry route on 15 February 1965. But this isn't quite the end of the story as a preservation group called the Foyle Valley Railway acquired a site just to the south of the former GNR(I) station site in Londonderry. A museum has been built and a 3 feet gauge line running some three miles south has been laid on the former trackbed. Services are operated by two former Co. Donegal railcars and it is hoped that the line will extend further south and across the border into Co. Tyrone.

Vernersbridge – Omagh

Passenger service withdrawn	15 February 1965
Distance	32.5 miles
Company	Great Northern Railway of Ireland

Stations closed	*Date*
Vernersbridge *	20 September 1954
Trew & Moy	15 February 1965
Shaw's Crossing **	1 October 1957
Dungannon (old station)	2 September 1861
Dungannon (new station) ***	15 February 1965
Dungannon Junction Crossing **	2 June 1958
Donaghmore	15 February 1965
Mullaghfurtherland Crossing **	13 June 1960

Stations closed	*Date*
Reynold's Crossing **	13 June 1960
Brimmage's **	13 June 1960
Pomeroy	15 February 1965
Carrickmore	1959
Rollingford Crossing **	13 June 1960
Sixmilecross ****	15 February 1965
Beragh	15 February 1965
Tattykernon Crossing **	13 June 1960
Edenderry Crossing **	13 June 1960
Garvaghy No. 1 Crossing **	13 June 1960
Garvaghy No. 2 Crossing **	13 June 1960
Omagh	15 February 1965

GNR(I) 0-6-0 QGs Class No. 152, 'Lurgan', stands at Dungannon Station with the 6.15 p.m. service to Cookstown, 13 April 1948. Four QG Class locomotives were built for the GNR(I) by the North British Locomotive Co. between 1903 and 1904.

* Formerly named Verner; renamed in December 1858.
** Railcar stopping place, opened in 1936/37.
*** Opened on 2 September 1861.
**** Opened in 1862.

Donaghmore Station.

The Portadown & Dungannon Railway was authorised in 1847 to build a line connecting the towns in its title and to ultimately connect to the Londonderry & Enniskillen Railway at Omagh by means of a later extension. The objective was to provide another through route from Belfast to Londonderry. The Belfast & Ballymena Railway, the Belfast, Ballymena, Coleraine & Portrush Junction Railway and the Londonderry & Coleraine Railway would eventually provide the other and remaining NCC route. The initial objective of the PDR was to reach Dungannon but nothing was done at first and it required a further Act of 1853 and financial assistance from the Ulster Railway to get things going again. Construction started in 1855 and in 1857 the company became the Portadown, Dungannon & Omagh Railway and started to extend to Omagh.

Work on the first section was completed in 1858 and the line was opened on 5 April 1858. The original terminus at Dungannon was a mile east of the later station. The extension started with an 814 yard long tunnel through a hill on the Northland Estate which was needed because the landowner, Lord Northland, objected to the smoke and fumes of passing trains. At the west end of the tunnel a permanent Dungannon Station was built. From Dungannon the line continued to Donaghmore, Pomeroy, Carrickmore, crossing bleak moorland, and then to Sixmilecross and Beragh. At the junction at Omagh the PDOR used the Londonderry & Enniskillen Railway station.

Sixmilecross Station.

The line was completed in 1861 and was officially opened to all traffic on 2 September 1861. The PDOR leased the line to the Ulster Railway for a period of 999 years, but as it turned out the lease only lasted until 1 January 1876 when the two companies amalgamated. In 1862 a half-mile branch was built at Omagh to serve the market. The branch left the mainline three quarters of a mile before Omagh Station at Market Branch Junction on the east side of the town, opening in June 1862.

GNR(I) PPs Class 4-4-0 No. 12 at Omagh, shunting a van from the 2.20 p.m. Belfast to Londonderry diesel set, 21 September 1957. Omagh is where the Derry Road met the Irish North and continued on to Londonderry.

On 1 April 1876 the Ulster Railway amalgamated with the short-lived Northern Railway to form the Great Northern Railway of Ireland. The new GNR(I) now owned and operated the line from Belfast as far as Omagh. The Londonderry & Enniskillen Railway were still the owners of the Omagh to Londonderry section and were paid a rent for the use of the line. This situation continued until 1883 when the LER amalgamated with the GNR(I), bringing the complete route from Belfast Great Victoria Street to Londonderry Foyle Road under the control of a single operator.

Just arriving at Omagh is GNR(I) Qs Class 4-4-0 No. 121, 'Pluto', with a Belfast to Londonderry service, 21 April 1948.

The Derry Road, as the line became known, was an important and busy link between the two major cities in Northern Ireland. In 1936 the GNR(I) introduced a railcar service on the line and in an effort to gain more trade these would stop at certain level crossings along the route. These railcar stops continued into UTA days, ceasing by 1960. After the formation of the Great Northern Railway Board in 1953 services continued to run as before, but this measure merely delayed the demise of Great Northern. On 1 October 1958 the company was disbanded and the assets split between CIE and the UTA. This section of line came under the control of the UTA and was destined to last only seven more years. Complete closure came on 15 February 1965.

Bundoran Junction – Bundoran

Passenger service withdrawn	1 October 1957		
Distance	35.25 miles		
Company	Great Northern Railway of Ireland		

Stations closed	*Date*	*Stations closed*	*Date*
Bundoran Junction	1 October 1957	Kesh	1 October 1957
Tague's Crossing *	1 October 1957	Pettigo	1 October 1957
Irvinestown	1 October 1957	Letter ***	date unknown
Johnston's Crossing *	by 1956	Leggs Crossing ***	date unknown
Castlearchdale Crossing *	by 1956	Castlecaldwell (old station)	August 1870
Drumadravy **	date unknown	Castlecaldwell (new station) ****	1 October 1957
Crowe's Crossing *	by 1956	Magherameenagh Castle *****	1 October 1957
		Belleek	1 October 1957
		Ballyshannon	1 October 1957
		Bundoran	1 October 1957

* Railcar stop from September 1934.
** Private station.
*** Stopping place for railcars to load or unload mailbags from nearby post office.
**** Opened in August 1870.
***** Private platform.

GNR(I) PPs Class 4-4-0, 'Sirocco', stands at Bundoran Junction Station with a train from Bundoran, 22 April 1953.

Irvinestown Station.

The Enniskillen & Bundoran Railway was incorporated on 11 July 1861 with the aim of building a railway from a junction at Lowtherstown on the Londonderry & Enniskillen Railway to Bundoran on the Co. Donegal coast. Just under a year later, on 30 June 1862, the company changed its name to the Enniskillen, Bundoran & Sligo Railway with powers to extend from Bundoran to Sligo. The intention was to use the Midland & Great Western Railway terminus at Sligo. The line opened on 13 June 1866 and was worked by the Irish North Western Railway who also happened to hold much of the capital. Despite a few attempts, the Sligo portion of the line was never built and Bundoran remained the terminus. Bundoran Junction had a direct curve provided in 1894 to allow trains from Omagh onto the branch without reversal.

Belleek Station. Belleek was famous for its pottery manufacture and a siding was provided by the railway to serve the pottery.

Although the INWR and L&ER had become part of the Great Northern Railway of Ireland in 1876 and 1883 respectively, the EB&SR remained independent, with services being worked by the GNR(I). The branch was eventually purchased by the GNR(I) in 1897, after some rather complicated legal difficulties. Bundoran had become a popular tourist resort and attracted many excursion trains, the GNR(I) also purchased a hotel in Bundoran in 1899, renaming it the Great Northern Hotel. Partition in 1921 caused problems for the branch, as it crossed the border three times, near Pettigo twice and at Belleek.

GNR(I) PPs Class 4-4-0 No. 46, 'Typhoon', stands by the signal box at Bundoran, 22 April 1953. Bundoran was a popular seaside resort and attracted a number of excursion trains. From 1943 the Bundoran Express was started, running from Dublin in the summer months.

This led to an interesting situation during the Second World War with the introduction of Double Summer Time in Northern Ireland in 1941 while the south remained on plain Summer Time. The 9.12 a.m. departure from Bundoran Junction would arrive at Pettigo at 8.47 a.m. and finally reached Bundoran at 9.30 a.m.! It did, of course, take rather longer than eighteen minutes to travel the thirty-five and a quarter miles. As with so many other GNR(I) lines, a railcar service was introduced in the 1930s, with the railcar making stops at various level crossings along the way. In 1943 the Bundoran Express was started, running in the summer months from Dublin, with non-stop running between Clones and Pettigo to avoid customs inspections. The fate of the branch was naturally tied to the main line and when this closed on 1 October 1957, the branch did too.

Dungannon – Cookstown

Passenger service withdrawn	16 January 1956
Distance	14.5 miles
Company	Great Northern Railway of Ireland

Stations closed	*Date*
Dungannon	15 February 1965
Dungannon Junction Crossing *	2 June 1958
Old Engine Crossing **	January 1942

Stations closed	*Date*
Coalisland	16 January 1956
Annagher Crossing **	January 1942
Lisnatrain Crossing **	January 1942
Stewartstown	16 January 1956
Grange Halt ***	January 1942
Killymoon Golf Links ****	1956
Cookstown	16 January 1956

GNR(I) 0-6-0 SG Class No. 178 heads the 3.00 p.m. departure from Dungannon to Cookstown in 1959. Goods services to Coalisland survived until 1965 with the line being worked as a siding from Dungannon.

* Railcar stopping place, opened in 1936/37 and remaining in use for Londonderry services until 2 June 1958.
** Railcar stopping place, opened in 1936/37.
*** Formerly Grange Crossing and replaced by a bridge *c.*1900. It became Grange Halt, a railcar stopping place, from 1936/37.
**** Opened in 1943.

Coalisland Station. The branch was closed from here to Cookstown in 1959. Goods services to Coalisland survived until 1965 with the line being worked as a siding from Dungannon.

The Belfast & Ballymena Railway had served Cookstown since 1856. However, in 1874 the Ulster Railway and the Portadown, Dungannon & Omagh Railway promoted the Dungannon & Cookstown Railway, their interest being in tapping into the coal deposits around Coalisland. Although construction had started, the line was still incomplete by the time the GNR(I) bought out the company in 1877.

Stewartstown Station lost its passenger services in 1956 with goods services surviving three more years until the closure of the line from Coalisland to Cookstown.

The Cookstown line left the PDOR line at Dungannon Junction, about half a mile from the second Dungannon Station. The line turned north to Coalisland and continued on to Stewartstown before reaching the terminus at Cookstown. The Dungannon & Cookstown station in Cookstown was adjacent to the Belfast & Ballymena station, although there was no facility for through running. However, an exchange siding for wagon transfers was provided. Construction work was completed in 1879 and the line opened for all traffic on 28 July 1879.

GNR(I) Ps Class 4-4-0 No. 89, 'Albert', stands on the turntable at Cookstown, 13 April 1948.

The line ran through an industrialised area of Northern Ireland, with numerous sidings serving various brickworks, sand quarries and collieries. A new coal mine was opened near Coalisland in 1924, but unfortunately the coal traffic did not come up to expectations and the coal was of poor quality. As with most other GNR(I) lines, a railcar service was introduced in the late 1930s, stopping at various level crossings along the way. The railcar stops didn't last very long, being discontinued from January 1942.

A 1936 view of Cookstown from above the NCC line. The GNR(I) line can be seen curving in from the left hand side of the picture.

In 1943 a halt was opened to serve Killymoon Golf Links, north of Stewartstown. The gradual demise of the line started in 1956 when passenger services were discontinued by the GNRB. The line passed to the control of the UTA in 1958 and a year later, on 5 January 1959, goods services were cut north of Coalisland with the line being worked as a siding. Dungannon Junction was taken out of use with the old down line being used for main line traffic and the old up line and Coalisland siding for sand traffic. The UTA's policy of discontinuing goods services saw the end of the line on 1 January 1965.

Fintona Junction – Fintona

Passenger service withdrawn	1 October 1957	*Stations closed*	*Date*
Distance	0.75 miles	Fintona Junction	1 October 1957
Company	Great Northern Railway of Ireland	Fintona	1 October 1957

The tram makes ready to depart Fintona Junction for the short run down to Fintona, 19 September 1929.

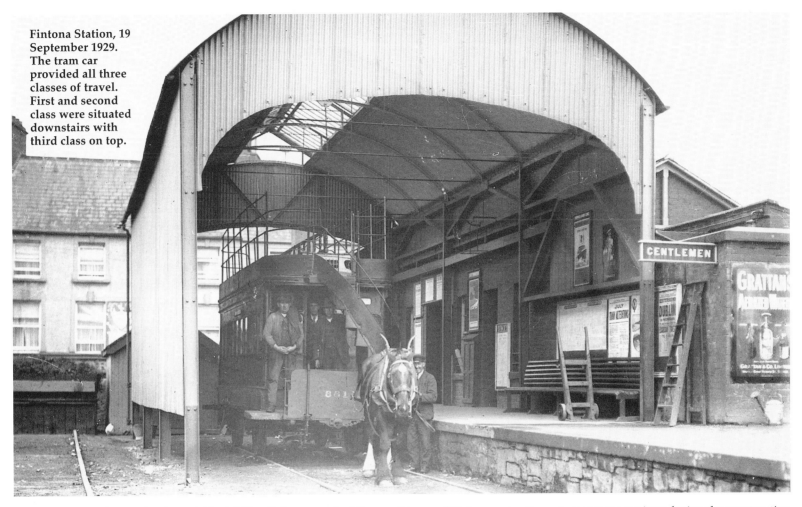

Fintona Station, 19 September 1929. The tram car provided all three classes of travel. First and second class were situated downstairs with third class on top.

On 15 June 1853 the Londonderry & Enniskillen Railway reached the small town of Fintona, using it as a temporary terminus during the construction of their line to Enniskillen. When the push south to Dromore Road commenced, it was decided to start the extension three quarters of a mile up the line from Fintona, leaving the town on a branch from 16 January 1854. The junction was provided with a station and was called, logically enough, Fintona Junction. The L&ER got permission from the Board of Trade to work the branch by horse, an arrangement that lasted for 104 years until closure. Steam engines were used for goods trains. Just two vehicles are thought to have been used on the line; the first from 1854 to 1883 was a double deck carriage.

Tram car No. 381 stands at Fintona Station. This was only the second tram car to be used on the branch in 104 years. Built in 1883 by the Metropolitan Company, it is now preserved at Cultra, Belfast.

The second vehicle was a replacement ordered from the Metropolitan Company and arrived in 1883. This four wheel tramcar had two compartments on the lower deck, divided into first and second class. The upper third class deck was open and was reached by two narrow spiral staircases, one at either end. In latter years, the motive power was provided by a horse called Dick. Unfortunately Dick was afraid of steam engines, so when the tram reached Fintona Junction he was unhitched and put into a shed next to the signal box until the steam engine had departed. The branch closed along with the rest of the Clones to Londonderry line on 1 October 1957. Fortunately, the tramcar was saved for preservation. It is interesting to note that in the 1950s the GNR(I) were operating steam, diesel, electric and horse-drawn services on their system, an eminent example of horses for courses!

Tynan – Maguiresbridge

Passenger service withdrawn	1 January 1942
Distance	37 miles
Company	Clogher Valley Railway

Stations closed	Date
Tynan	1 January 1942
Caledon	1 January 1942
Kilsampson	1 January 1942
Ramaket	1 January 1942
Emyvale Road *	1 January 1942
Cumber	1 January 1942
Glenkeen	1 January 1942

Stations closed	Date
Crilly	1 January 1942
Glencrew	1 January 1942
Aughnacloy	1 January 1942
Stormhill	1889
Tullyvar	1 January 1942
Ballygawley	1 January 1942
Lisdoort	1 January 1942
Annaghilla	1 January 1942
Roughan	1 January 1942
Augher	1 January 1942
Farranetra **	1 January 1942

* Opened as Curlagh or Curlough; renamed in July 1896.
** Also called Summer Hill.

Aughnacloy was the headquarters of the Clogher Valley Railway and also housed the main maintenance facilities for the railway. Two Sharp, Stewart 0-4-2Ts, No. 6, 'Erne', and No. 2, 'Errigal', stand with ex-Castlederg & Victoria Bridge Tramway 2-6-2T No. 4, 18 August 1939.

Tynan – Maguiresbridge (continued)

Stations closed	Date	Stations closed	Date
Clogher	1 January 1942	Killarbran	1 January 1942
Carryclogher	1 January 1942	Claraghey ***	1 January 1942
Findermore	1 January 1942	Colebrooke	1 January 1942
Ballagh	1 January 1942	Stonepark ***	1 January 1942
Kiltermon	1 January 1942	Skeog *	1 January 1942
Ballyvadden *	1 January 1942	Brookeborough	1 January 1942
Fivemiletown	1 January 1942	Aghavea	1 January 1942
Cranbrooke	1 January 1942	Maguiresbridge Fair Green	1 January 1942
Tattyknuckle **	1897	Maguiresbridge	1 January 1942
Corrylongford	1 January 1942		

CVR 0-4-2T No. 6, 'Erne', at Aughnacloy with the 4.05 p.m. Fivemiletown to Tynan service, 18 September 1929.

* Opened in November 1887.
** Opened 8 April 1890; omitted from timetables from 15 April 1897.
*** Opened in 1926.

Although the CVR was a roadside tramway for much of its route, it did provide a few stations that were more like conventional railway buildings such as Ballygawley.

The Clogher Valley is an area of south Tyrone consisting of numerous small towns and villages that were engaged in agriculture, textiles manufacturing, brewing, and other light industries, mainly centred around Clogher. It must be said, though, that the area wasn't known as the Clogher Valley until the coming of the railway. Various schemes had been mooted to connect the area to other railways being built. The Portadown, Dungannon & Omagh Railway had planned a 5 feet 3 inch gauge branch from Dungannon to Aughnacloy in 1861, but nothing came of it.

In an effort to cut costs the CVR purchased a diesel railcar from Walker Brothers of Wigan in 1932. When the railway closed, Railcar 1 was purchased by the Co. Donegal and became their No. 10. Fortunately, it survived the breakers' yard and is now preserved at Cultra, Belfast.

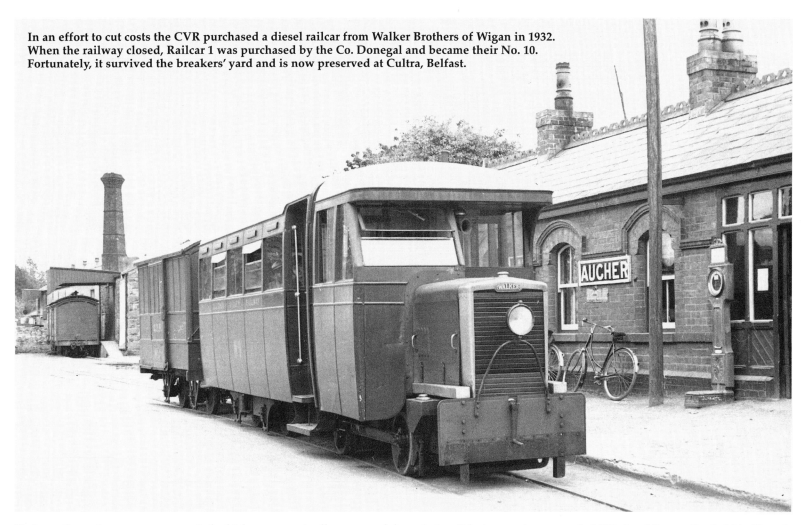

Various other schemes were promoted which were eventually narrowed down to two 3 feet gauge tramways in 1883. A public meeting held in Omagh in September 1883 discussed these two proposals. Both schemes were planned to start at Maguiresbridge on the GNR(I) Dundalk to Enniskillen line and continue to Fivemiletown, Clogher and Ballygawley. From here the routes differed, one group wanted to go to Dungannon, whereas the other wanted to go to Tynan. A split inevitably occurred, which led to the Tyrone Steam Tramways pushing ahead with its plans to go to Dungannon.

A busy scene at Clogher Station as No. 3, 'Blackwater', with the 10.45 a.m. service from Tynan, passes Railcar 1 (and van number 5) with the 12.00 noon service from Fivemiletown, 25 June 1937.

This scheme failed to get support from the Tyrone Grand Jury, which left the way open for the Clogher Valley Tramways to go to Tynan. The company was incorporated in December 1883 and having secured Baronial Guarantees from both the Tyrone and Fermanagh Grand Juries, construction started in 1885. The line was ready for inspection in April 1887 and was duly approved. The line officially opened for traffic on 2 May 1887. At Tynan the tramway used the GNR(I) station and ran by the side of the road for much of the route westwards.

Railcar 1 and its van make their way through Main Street, Fivemiletown. At some 388 feet above sea level, Main Street was the highest point on the CVR.

Aughnacloy was the headquarters of the tramway and had quite an impressive station, more in keeping with a proper railway than a roadside tramway. Maintenance facilities for locomotives and rolling stock were also provided here. Continuing westwards the tramway reached Fivemiletown where the trains made their way through the main street. From Fivemiletown to Maguiresbridge the tramway mainly used its own right of way. The end of the line was at the GNR(I) station at Maguiresbridge.

Fivemiletown Station, 25 June 1937. Having passed through Main Street, the railway swung off the road and into the station. The station building faced Main Street.

Not surprisingly, this was yet another tramway that failed to make any money. Nevertheless, this did not deter the owners from considering expanding the system. One scheme, proposed in 1891, harked back to earlier days by promoting the building of a branch from Ballygawley to Dungannon. In 1894, still in expansionist mood, the company changed its name to the Clogher Valley Railway. Other schemes sought to build a narrow gauge line from Clifden to Newry, using parts of the Cavan & Leitrim Railway, the Clogher Valley and the Bessbrook & Newry Tramway.

CVR No. 6, 'Erne', with van number 4 and carriage number 12, at Fivemiletown with the 9.50 a.m. Maguiresbridge to Tynan service, 25 June 1937.

Despite getting an Act in 1903, the Ulster & Connaught Light Railway, promoters of the scheme, failed to build anything. Meanwhile, the Clogher Valley Railway continued to lose money until a government investigation in 1927 saw the imposition of management committee which was appointed by Tyrone and Fermanagh county councils.

No. 6, 'Erne', pauses for custom at Stoneparkcross with the 9.50 a.m. service from Maguiresbridge, 25 June 1937. Most of the CVR's stops were like this one with a bench, nameboard and noticeboard being the only provisions.

Included on this committee was Henry Forbes of the Co. Donegal Railway. His influence saw a revitalisation of the CVR, including the purchase of a diesel railcar and a rail lorry, the shortening of journey times and the introduction of more services. However, competition from road services increased and the line continued to lose money until eventually the government, which had become the major shareholder by this time, had no option but to close the line.

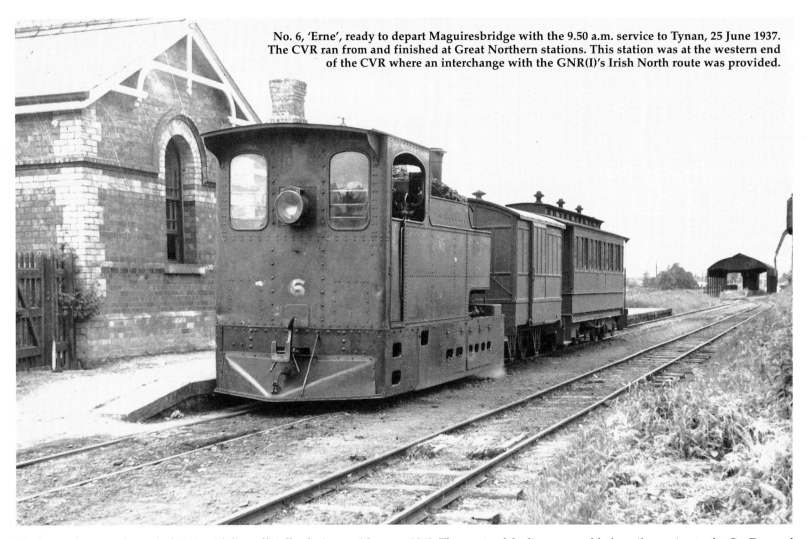

No. 6, 'Erne', ready to depart Maguiresbridge with the 9.50 a.m. service to Tynan, 25 June 1937. The CVR ran from and finished at Great Northern stations. This station was at the western end of the CVR where an interchange with the GNR(I)'s Irish North route was provided.

The last train ran at the end of 1941, with line officially closing on 1 January 1942. The assets of the line were sold, the railcar going to the Co. Donegal Railway, becoming their railcar No. 10 which is now preserved. Some of the wagons went to the Cavan & Leitrim section of the Great Southern Railway and a few more to Bord na Móna.

Victoria Bridge – Castlederg

Passenger service withdrawn	17 April 1933	*Stations closed*	*Date*
Distance	7 miles	Crew	17 April 1933
Company	Castlederg & Victoria Bridge Tramway	Fyfin	17 April 1933
		Stonewalls	by 1895
Stations closed	*Date*	Glen *	by 1928
Castlederg	17 April 1933	Victoria Bridge	17 April 1933
Spamount	17 April 1933		* Opened *c.*1912/13; closure date unknown.

Castlederg looking east, 6 August 1930. No. 4, a Hudswell, Clarke 2-6-0T stands on the left while No. 5, a Hudswell, Clarke 0-4-4T, arrives with a train from Victoria Bridge.

When the Londonderry & Enniskillen Railway opened their line from Strabane to Newtownstewart in 1852, the company passed by the town of Castlederg some seven miles to the west. The nearest station was Victoria Bridge and inevitably the people of Castlederg started to consider some form of connection to the main line. A number of schemes were proposed, initially broad gauge, but by the early 1880s the proposals had been narrowed down to one for a 3 feet gauge roadside tramway. The bill was passed in July 1883 and construction commenced. The line was ready for opening the next year and a Board of Trade inspection on 5 July 1884 found the line fit for use. The official opening of the line occurred five days later with much pomp and ceremony. Public services started the following day. At Castlederg, a spur left the rear of the station to serve the market place.

Spamount Station. This Beyer, Peacock 2-4-0T locomotive was ex-Ballymena & Larne Railway No. 105, bought in 1928 for £225 from the NCC. The locomotive never actually displayed a number but was generally regarded as No. 3.

Travelling east, the tramway climbed for one and three quarter miles up to Spamount Halt and from there the ascent continued for a further one and a quarter miles to Crew halt. Interestingly, an Ordnance Survey map refers to the halt as Crew Station and, needless to say, there were many jokes made about the confusion of this station and a slightly larger one in Cheshire! The line continued to climb to the summit some 300 feet above sea level at about four and half miles out. The line then started its descent to Victoria Bridge, stopping at Fyfin halt. Continuing downhill, the tramway then came to two unstaffed halts. The first at Stonewalls opened with the line while the second at Glen seems to have been in use by 1912 or 1913 – neither appeared in Bradshaw. From Glen the descent continued into Victoria Bridge Station where the tramway terminated in a curving bay platform behind the Great Northern down platform. Business was initially good. The First World War scarcely affected the tramway apart from increased agricultural traffic mainly consisting of potatoes going to the city markets. However, after the war it found itself under competition from lorries and cars. Profits began to fall and increased competition in the form of buses began in the mid-1920s.

Partition in 1921 didn't help the tramway as customs inspections hindered traffic. In an effort to run services more economically, an internal combustion-engined railcar was considered as one had been successful on the neighbouring Co. Donegal Railway. Although a quote had been obtained from England, the company decided to build their own paraffin-engined railcar. Underpowered and with a long wheelbase, the railcar was used from 1925 to 1928 and ended up costing more than the English quote! The British coal strike of 1926 caused severe problems, the price of coal increasing fivefold. However, the company was still able to use their railcar which saw them through the worst of the problems. Despite these efforts, the tramway continued to lose money and by 1932 it had become insolvent. The final blow came with the 1933 Railway Strike which led to services being suspended. Although the strike ended on 8 April, the company decided to call it a day and never resumed services, the line being officially closed on 17 April that year. The company was officially wound up on 30 September 1933 and the assets were disposed of. A locomotive and some wagons went to the Clogher Valley Railway and the railcar went to the Co. Donegal Railway where it was rebuilt as Railcar No. 2.

Strabane – Londonderry Victoria Road *

Passenger service withdrawn	1 January 1955	**Stations closed**	**Date**
Distance	14.5 miles	Ballymagorry	1 January 1955
Company	Northern Counties Committee	Ballyheather Halt **	1 January 1955
		Donemana	1 January 1955
Stations closed	**Date**	Cullion	1 January 1955
Strabane	1 January 1955	Desertone Halt ***	1 January 1955

One of the six Class 2 4-6-0T locomotives built by Neilson in 1893, pictured at Strabane.

* The closed stations on this line that were in Co. Derry were New Buildings and Londonderry Victoria Road.
** Opened in 1902.
*** Opened in 1908.

The narrow gauge railways in Co. Donegal, eventually known as the Co. Donegal Railways Joint Committee, converged at Strabane where there was an interchange with the Great Northern Railway of Ireland, passengers having to change platforms and goods being transhipped between broad and narrow gauges before reaching their destinations. Because of this situation a scheme was promoted in the 1890s to build a narrow gauge line from Strabane to Londonderry. The proposal met with stiff opposition from the GNR(I) who claimed that the line would duplicate their existing route, but despite this an Act was obtained in 1896 for the Donegal Railway to build its own line to Londonderry.

Strabane narrow gauge station during the floods of 1909. The Co. Donegal Railway terminated here until the Londonderry extension was opened in 1900.

Construction commenced and the fourteen and a half mile line was opened for goods traffic on 1 August 1900 and for passengers five days later. Leaving Strabane, the line continued north for a short distance before turning north-east, crossing over the GNR(I) line and continuing up the east side of the River Foyle through the counties of Tyrone and Londonderry, leaving the GNR(I) on the Co. Donegal side of the river. The Donegal Railway terminus in Londonderry was at Victoria Road, a short distance south of the BNCR Waterside station and next to the Carlisle Bridge. The Londonderry Port & Harbour Commissioners built their own mixed gauge railway, connecting the Donegal Railway with the BNCR to the north, and across the lower deck of the bridge to the GNR(I) Foyle Road station, on the opposite side of the river, and to the Londonderry & Lough Swilly Railway's Graving Dock station. In 1903 the English Midland Railway entered the scene when they purchased the Belfast & Northern Counties Railway. Keen to expand elsewhere, the MR approached the Donegal Railway with a view to purchasing it. Alarmed at the prospect, the GNR(I) understandably objected to the proposal. Agreement was finally reached in 1906 whereby both the GNR(I) and the MR jointly purchased the company and set up the Co. Donegal Railways Joint Committee to manage the system. However, Parliament was concerned that the GNR(I) would have a monopoly on the Londonderry to Strabane route and consequently the narrow gauge route passed entirely to the Midland Railway Northern Counties Committee with the line being worked by the CDRJC. The MR NCC became the LMS NCC in 1924.

Railcar No. 7 with trailer No. 2 at the platform of Strabane narrow gauge station, 20 April 1948. Introduced in 1930, this railcar was the first with a diesel engine to enter service on a railway in the British Isles.

The fortunes of the CDRJC started to decline in the years between the wars despite economies such as the extensive introduction of railcars. The Second World War had more of an effect on the line. Londonderry became an important naval base and generated a lot of war traffic. However, this was routed over the NCC route to Waterside station via Coleraine because the GNR(I) route passed through several miles of neutral Éire and the narrow gauge was considered unsuitable because of transhipment difficulties at Strabane. The NCC passed to the control of the Ulster Transport Authority on 1 April 1949, although it continued to be worked by the CDRJC. The UTA were not disposed to subsidise loss-making railways and issued a notice in October 1954 stating their intentions to withdraw services on the line. It closed to all traffic on 1 January 1955. However, due to a UTA bus strike, one last train was run on 30 June 1955, a Sunday school excursion from Strabane to Portrush.

Enniskillen – Belcoo & Black Lion

Passenger service withdrawn	1 October 1957		*Stations closed*	*Date*
Distance	12 miles		Enniskillen *	1883
Company	Sligo, Leitrim & Northern Counties Railway		Mullaghy **	by 1918
			Florencecourt	1 October 1957
Stations closed	*Date*		Abohill **	1 October 1957
Enniskillen	1 October 1957		Belcoo & Black Lion ***	1 October 1957

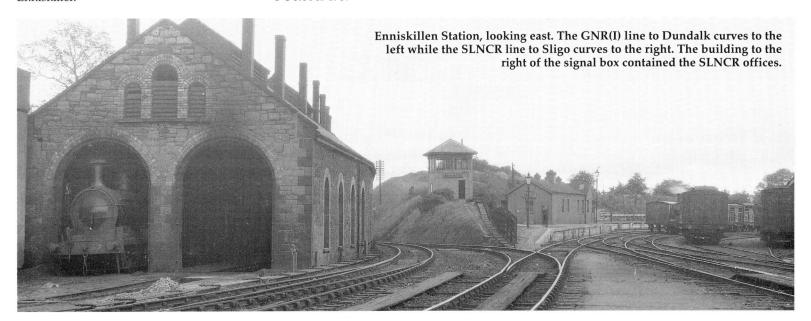

Enniskillen Station, looking east. The GNR(I) line to Dundalk curves to the left while the SLNCR line to Sligo curves to the right. The building to the right of the signal box contained the SLNCR offices.

Sligo was connected to the railway system in 1862 when the Midland & Great Western Railway extended their line from Longford. However, various landowners and prominent citizens of the area were keen to provide a rail connection serving Co. Sligo, Co. Leitrim and on to Londonderry and Belfast. The idea was to provide another outlet for livestock traffic other than the MGWR route to Dublin. An Act was duly passed on 11 August 1875 authorising the Sligo, Leitrim & Northern Counties Railway to build a line from a junction with the MGWR at Ballysodare to a junction with the Irish North Western Railway at Enniskillen. The SLNCR were also to have running powers over the MGWR line from Ballysodare into Sligo and over the Sligo Quay goods branch, as well as over a short distance of the INWR line into the passenger station at Enniskillen. Construction started in 1877 from the Enniskillen end and the line was built as cheaply as possible. The resultant railway was abundant in heavy gradients, sharp curves, numerous level crossings, and steep sided cuttings and embankments which were prone to landslides.

* Temporary terminus from 1879 to 1883.   ** Opened in 1886.   *** Formerly Belcoo; renamed Belcoo & Black Lion in 1908.

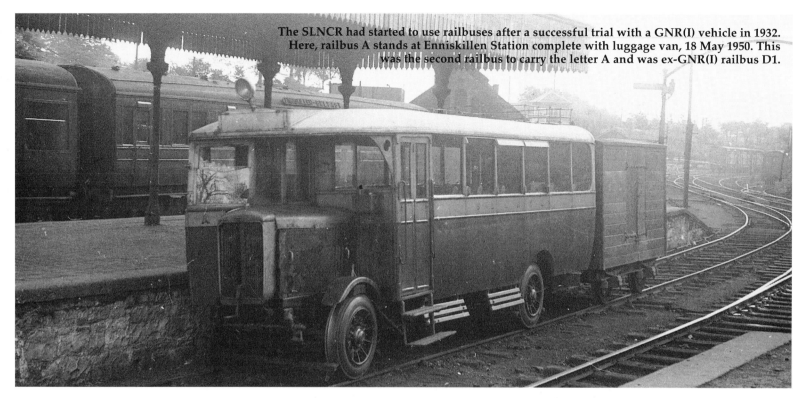

The SLNCR had started to use railbuses after a successful trial with a GNR(I) vehicle in 1932. Here, railbus A stands at Enniskillen Station complete with luggage van, 18 May 1950. This was the second railbus to carry the letter A and was ex-GNR(I) railbus D1.

The first section of line, from Enniskillen to Belcoo, was ready for opening in early 1879 and goods traffic commenced on 12 February 1879. The Board of Trade inspected the line on 4 March and after a few alterations the line opened to passenger traffic on 18 March 1879. Up until 1883 the SLNCR used their own temporary station at Enniskillen. Although the SLNCR intended to use the GNR(I) station, it took until 1883 before agreement was reached with the GNR(I) over the layout of the junction. However, a junction of some form was provided for wagon transfer. The major engineering feature of the line was just outside Enniskillen Station. The SLNCR had to cross the River Erne and did so by the 467 feet, eight span Weir's Bridge (sometimes referred to as Killyhevlin Bridge). From here the line continued for five and a quarter miles to Florencecourt and then on to Belcoo. Two intermediate stations were opened in 1886, one at Mullaghy (four and a half miles) and another at Abohill (eight and a quarter miles). Mullaghy was closed by 1918. At Belcoo the line crossed the River MacNean into Co. Leitrim. The extension of the line towards Sligo was built piecemeal, requiring a loan from the Board of Works to complete. However, the line was eventually completed and opened for traffic throughout on 7 November 1882. Financial troubles beset the line from the beginning and came to a head in 1890 when a receiver was appointed. Although by 1894 income had improved, unsatisfactory repayment of the BoW loan meant that the Treasury was seriously considering selling the line to the MGWR and GNR(I). Opposition to the sale of the line was mounted by the SLNCR, the mayor of Sligo and at least fifteen MPs. The Treasury eventually agreed to financial restructuring of the company and the SLNCR was brought out of receivership in 1897.